STAYING *Attached* TO THE VINE

By

The Rev. Angela C. Bosfield Palacious

Staying Attached to the Vine

ISBN: 15-6229812

The Scripture passages were all taken from *The New Revised Standard Version* of the Bible unless otherwise indicated.

First published 2010

Angela Palacious Ministries

P.O. Box N. 4553
Nassau, Bahamas
Telephone: 242-393-9000
angelapalacious@yahoo.com

Also by Rev. Angela Palacious

Medley of Meditations
Seasons of the Church
Praying with and for Children
Walking in the Spirit
Allowing the Scriptures to Speak
Oasis in the Desert Vol. 1
Oasis in the Desert CDs Vol. 1-7
Sharing Our Stories of Encounters with God
Entering God's Presence (cassette)
Praying with and for Children (cassette)

READERS' RESPONSES

As always, your writings are inspirational and encouraging. Your breathing exercises are quite helpful and when followed, result in a calming effect. You have included situations that everyone can identify with. May you continue to be a blessing through sharing your knowledge and experience with others.

Mary Mycklewhyte

Again, I have to say how impressed I am, Angela, with your writings. The most striking feature, I feel, is that you speak from your heart directly to the reader's heart, and that is powerful stuff. So often, a reader will thump a cushion and say 'yes!' or will wince as another arrow finds its mark! You have a wonderful talent and I'm sure your family and all your readers appreciate that!

Josie Chapman

I have been blessed by your book. While I examined it, it examined me. I was ministered to and inspired while I sifted through your words. I thank you.

Obediah Smith

PREFACE

By The Grace of God
To The Glory of God

Some of these meditations were written for airing on radio, others were written for church bulletins and newspaper. They are presented as reflections on life as seen through the eyes of a Bahamian Christian.

It is my prayer that those who heard or read them in the past find this book a helpful reminder of some favourite pieces, and that those who are not acquainted with them will enjoy being challenged by these thoughts for the first time. May you be blessed and live to be a real blessing to others in your generation and for those yet unborn.

Angela Bosfield Palacious
October 11, 2009
Nassau, Bahamas

ACKNOWLEDGEMENTS

Grateful thanks and all honour and glory go to my Saviour and Lord, Jesus Christ, whose resurrected life makes it possible for me to be alive in the Spirit. Sincere gratitude is extended to the members of the Bahamian public, who read my weekly articles and especially to all those Christians of all denominations and walks of life who offer prayerful support.

The meditations on Junkanoo were inspired by the wonderful book *I Come to Get Me,* written by my extremely talented cousin Arlene Nash Ferguson. *Getting Down to Business* meditations were written after speaking with former parishioner Matthew Mitchell. The beautiful photographs of grapes were taken by our good friend Michael Bullard (now deceased) in a vineyard which he, his wife Gaynell, my husband and I visited in Chile. Ron Clarke gave needed technical advice and assistance with the selection of the pictures.

I have been greatly assisted by the editing efforts of my former GCE high school teacher Josie Chapman (1964-68), my parishioner and rector's wife Mary Mycklewhyte, my Thursday parishioner Obediah Smith, and my dear husband, Jimmy.

God bless you all!

TABLE OF CONTENTS

INTRODUCTION

The Vine and the Branches

"I am the true vine, and my Father is the gardener. He cuts off every branch in me that bears no fruit, while every branch that does bear fruit he prunes so that it will be even more fruitful. You are already clean because of the word I have spoken to you. Remain in me, and I will remain in you. No branch can bear fruit by itself; it must remain in the vine. Neither can you bear fruit unless you remain in me". (John 15:1-4 NIV)

For many people these are difficult times for a variety of reasons. There are those who have been experiencing emotional disconnection as a result of economic hardship, unemployment, arid and unfulfilling relationships, grief and losses as well as spiritual isolation when apathy or emptiness make each day a weary repetition of the dull and mundane.

We all need a place of refreshment, and a time to be renewed or re-directed. Meditating provides an excellent opportunity to organize priorities and gain strength by celebrating our attachment to The Vine of Jesus Christ.

It is my hope that these few minutes that we have together will be like a time to drink deeply from inner springs so that we may thrive like plants in a well-watered garden. Otherwise, we wither and fade; we have "dry spells" and "rough patches"; we become "stressed out" and "burned out," unless we invite some degree of balance, by allowing the sap of The Vine to sustain us.

An orchard is a place where plants are nurtured by a loving gardener. A grape arbour offers shade from the sun, rest for the weary, and hope for the journey. May this book be an arbour for you every time you read it, and may you always stay attached to The Vine.

God bless you.

PART I

STAYING ATTACHED TO THE VINE AS AN INDIVIDUAL

Chapter One
HOW TO PRAY

How to Pray—Part 1

This relationship is a free gift to everyone, so there is no favouritism here. Even the smallest child or the oldest person can find a place around the throne of grace.

Little ones may be taught to kneel as a sign of respect. It settles the body in an unusual posture that allows the head to bow when eyes are closed without fear of falling over. It is an act of humility to lower oneself into a position of inferiority, even as we curtsy or bow in the presence of a king or queen.

Standing to pray was a regular Jewish custom. This allows the head to also be bowed, and a rocking motion is often a sign of the intensity and fervour of the prayer. Raised arms need firmly planted feet, and so a different kind of giving up of oneself is modelled in this position.

When we sit in a chair to meditate, contemplate or pray the scriptures, it enables us to be lost in wonder, love and praise for long periods of time. Sometimes we sleep and wake, and we are still in the posture of prayer. Of course, if this becomes a regular habit soon after prayer time begins, you may need to move to a different posture that promotes a more alert response.

Flat on the floor is a dramatic representation of the highest honour, or it may indicate the heaviness of one's heart. Lying flat on one's back at the beach or in the grass is a wonderful way to consider the glory of the sky be it night or day. Lying on one's stomach permits the reading of a book or prayer, or the close inspection of small creatures in the grass or sand.

Then there are the slow undulating steps of the one who is dancing in the arms of the Lord, or the whirling of oneself in exalted praise. Liturgical dance in the privacy of one's home allows the scriptures to come alive as Miriam celebrates the crossing of the Red Sea, or David dances after war or the healed leaps in praise of God. If your child were raised from the dead what do you think you would do?

Some pray as they exercise, or walk, or shower, and definitely while driving or doing manual work.

All of these are postures or positions to help you focus on this wonderful relationship. God will guide you and in this case if it feels good, then do it. Together you will enjoy every time you choose to pray in any way.

How to Pray – Part II

Once you decide on your body position, the next step is the method of prayer. Again you have so many choices.

Breath prayers, as I have mentioned before, are so easy and natural for even the smallest child or sickest patient. Acknowledge God as you breathe in and fill yourself with the sense of God's presence, releasing everything to God as you exhale. You may pray about your finances and remain calm. Offer God all relationships and remain at peace. Breathe and think and pray, as often as you can throughout the day. Keep God on your mind as much as you can. It will keep you in touch with the power of the Holy One.

Call on the name of Jesus, or some other title of God (e.g. Vine or Shepherd) to introduce the scriptures that you know, especially if you need the healing of memories. Such prayers intentionally invite the presence of Jesus into your situation to heal, forgive, challenge, and transform. Recall the exact details and let Jesus change the spiritual outcome for you. How you remember it will be healed, so that the negative effect may be cancelled eventually.

Counting your blessings one by one is a fascinating exercise, if you do it in writing. Before long, full pages will emerge as you take time to really focus on the advantages you enjoy: relationships, experiences, physical parts of the body that work and internal organs that function. If you start to number your possessions as if taking inventory, what about that for a way to pray!

Writing in a journal is a documentation of truth as you experience it: thoughts and feelings, hopes and dreams, discoveries and experiments, mistakes and failures, successes and triumphs, adventures and escapades. Your whole life will take on freshness as you remember that you will have to give an account of your use of time.

Try the following approaches: Prayers of adoration, confession, thanksgiving, and supplication (ACTS), as well as silence (when enough has been said) to just listen, learn and enjoy. Try reading about prayer to deepen understanding, followed by a time of personal prayer.

What a wonderful buffet of how to pray. You can approach the Lord in a different way every day as long as you are faithful and follow the Spirit's guidance on how to pray starting today.

How to Pray – Part III

Alone with your thoughts you establish intimacy. Undisturbed and unhurried, at peace and at rest in a comfortable position, your Sabbath time with the Lord can literally last all day.

With a prayer partner, you came in agreement on whatever is pleasing to God as far as you can tell. You open your heart, accountable to another. You are encouraged and criticized with loving directions. You inspire each other to greatness, and you believe in each other's inner beauty. Any friendship moves to a new level when both partners know how to pray, or one can teach the other. Couples who truly humble themselves before the Lord feel less inclined to humiliate each other in public.

A group gathered for Morning Prayer, Evening Prayer, Compline or extempore prayer possesses power to create community in a different way. This gathering speaks of corporate worship among the faithful, and establishes a firm foundation for a family, workplace, cell group, or any other configuration.

A classroom is transformed by the Spirit of God when teachers pray, and will be even more if all the students are adding their prayer to the activities of the day. An office or business becomes a place of wisdom and love if several people start to pray in earnest throughout the day. There is power in persistent prayer.

So much electricity is generated in a room full of praying people! So much more in a stadium or huge hotel ballroom that has been prepared in advance by those sent to pray! When all are gathered together by hundreds or thousands it is like dynamite. Prayers on the web, or the internet, or television for millions to participate, surely such prayer has to change the world.

Don't hold back on your power. Log on to your spiritual life. Decide right now where and when you will pray for devotional time each day, what form you will use, and then be faithful. It is no secret that God expects you to pray, as Jesus says in Matthew 6:5, "When you pray". In Matthew 18:19, he speaks of it being "in my name". Pray for a heart to pray, to follow God's way and that will keep you praying for the rest of this day.

When to Pray

When to pray may be your first question. I cannot imagine a time that is not a good time for you to pray. As soon as you open your eyes think, "Thank you, Lord, I have a mind and can pray" or "This is the day that the Lord has made, I will rejoice and be glad in it".

Let your mind begin to praise God for all the blessings of the past day and the peaceful rest, even as you offer your new day back to God. You may read and pray at this time, before you begin your morning regimen. There is always time to acknowledge your Creator if only for a few minutes.

A simple procedure like washing your face may become a spiritual reminder of how your sins have been washed away. Cleaning your teeth invites you to remember to use your mouth to call on the name of the Lord. Dressing may speak to you of being clothed in the garments of righteousness or putting on spiritual armour.

When you eat you may give thanks for food and ongoing provisions as well as reflecting on the body and blood of Christ which nourish you spiritually. Just a glance through a window enables you to reflect on the beauty of creation and the gift of life. A drive in a car or bus or a walk along the street provides an opportunity to pray for safety for yourself and others.

As you think of each member of your family, say a prayer for them as soon as they cross your mind, and that goes for friends, colleagues and even perfect strangers whom you meet.

All through the day, you may say that you are sorry for mistakes in judgment, hasty words, hard-hearted attitudes and anything else, even as you accept the forgiveness that always accompanies a sincere confession.

Bedtime is review time to do examination of conscience, counting of blessings and a bringing of closure to the day by praying for your enemies or those who behave that way.

When all is said and done, all day everyday is a good time to pray. You may repeat that until you really believe it and apply it: "all day everyday is a good time to pray".

YOUR REFLECTIONS

CHAPTER TWO
THE SUMMER

Relax

Take time this summer to think about who you are, and who you used to be, and what you have let slip out of your view as you started to go the other way. Renew some of your childhood promises to make a difference in the world, and watch your banner of priorities in life start once more to unfurl.

As I follow my own advice, I am sitting on a patio in the mountains of Asheville, North Carolina, where in front of me is a lake with water lilies and around me are huge pine trees with a breeze blowing through them that makes it sound as if I am near the sea. If I close my eyes, I could be on one of our Bahamian beaches; instead I am in a different kind of tranquility.

Relax, unwind, let go, slow down, be still—all words that order us to change our pace. This is the time when school comes to an end, vacations usually begin and fewer meetings are held. It is a time when we are called to take better care of ourselves.

What is it that you would like to do if you could convince yourself that you had done all that you "had" to do? What would bring a smile to your face to just think about having a chance to do it?

When last did you sit on your porch or patio and watch the world go by? When last have you 'rocked' in a rocking chair until you fell asleep? When last have you rocked in a hammock or just lay there quite still watching insects or enjoyed the sensation of elevating your feet?

Everything has its season - if you are an "uptight" sort of person why don't you ask God to help you to "loosen your grip"? Do things a little differently. Why don't you relax and allow slower rhythms and a change of scene to help you to feel renewed? If you renew a subscription it means you agree to have the deliveries start all over again. What in your life was a good thing you used to subscribe to that needs to be renewed deliberately every now and again?

Revive

Summer is a time to revive relationships that you cherish. What were some of the family outings that you used to enjoy all together, or a gathering of the large clan?

Did you have a games night in your home, or someone else's, where you drank soft drinks, played board games, talked about old memories and had clean and wholesome fun? What about no T.V. and DVD and computer games for one week, and get together with your neighbours and have a pot-luck party in the street?

Gather together more often with elderly relatives (before it is the funeral wake) and look through old family albums that you each bring, and let the past come alive for your children, before it is too late.

Think of some things that you will hate to miss if you could no longer drive, see, or hear, and invite them back into your life. When you get older you need not regret that if you had realized how much of life you were missing, you would have changed your pace.

What are some of the things you would like to do to make your life more enjoyable?Don't wait until you near your time to die to discover that you never really lived.

Refill

Some restaurants offer free drink refills; consider this meditation an invitation to accept a free refill of your empty spiritual cup. For example, are you getting low on love? Has life made you withdraw, become angry or bitter, a bit of a recluse? Lift up your cup for a refill of God's love. Let the love of the Lord bless you once more with the sweet froth of affection and tenderness, then become a blessing in some way each day.

Are you diminishing in your capacity to experience joy? Is it more difficult to smile, much less laugh, or are you becoming a "wet blanket," actually a real "kill-joy"? Lift your cup to be refilled with the bubbles of a buoyant spirit: Do something that makes you feel like a child; blow some bubbles; draw with crayons; just be silly and giggle, or let out a guffaw. Remember that happiness is fleeting but the joy of the Lord lasts for evermore.

Are you depleted of peace or spiritually restless? Ask the Spirit to teach you how to surrender the problems, and relax in the love that will help you to pass the peace test. Hold up your cup for the peace of the Lord to start to pour within you.

Are you running low on goodness, to do what you know is right, ranging from life- style to work ethic, from relationships with others and yourself, and especially your relationship with God? Then, hold up your cup for more goodness to make you more secure. We need you to set a better example so that others may live a life of goodness too.

Are you losing your gentleness, becoming harsh and hard to please? Do you push people around, and raise your voice and leave them spiritually wounded and feeling despondent? Nice and easy does it. Start to take your time. Be gentle and gracious. Pray to help others get through the tough times by your gentle guiding light.

Is your faith weakening? Are you less trusting in God than you used to be? Lift the cup of your heart to the one who died to prove God's love.

Look at the cross and remember that suffering and injustice were a part of his life. His resurrection contains the promise of our resurrection, and joy is going to come one of these mornings.

Is your meekness hard to handle? Is it difficult to wait on the Lord and not dictate how everything must be? Ask God for the strength to bite your tongue or speak your truth in real love, for patience to wait and for self-control. All have to come from above.

Use the summer, or any time, to relax, to be renewed and revived by having the cup of your soul refilled.

YOUR REFLECTIONS

Chapter Three
LONG JOURNEYS

Travel

There seems to be such restlessness in the human spirit that makes us want to move from where we are to arrive at some place new. Actually, not all of us are excited by the thought of distant travel. There are some who have lived in one place all of their lives and would rather not go beyond their own known territory. Now that travel is faster and the remotest places are accessible, more people are willing to experience other cultures. That was before September 11, 2001. There has been a shift in general enthusiasm since the reality of terrorism invaded the western hemisphere.

Traffic fatalities, on American highways for example, have drawn our attention to the dangers involved in movement abroad. A car accident can happen anywhere, at anytime, and our own local statistics force us to realize that we may as well say our prayers to calm our fears, and enjoy God's planet earth.

The thought of locking up the house, paying off bills that may become due in our absence, arranging for the care of pets, and all the other details involved in travel for lengthy periods of time, just the thought may put some of us off. Nevertheless, if we don't get away, usually we end up working more than we should so we can't win either way. We may as well expend the energy, plan our departure, and vacate the scene.

Our Lord went up in the mountains to pray, crossed the lake in a boat, walked to new towns and villages. He was working as he went, but I am sure he also enjoyed the change.

If we use the metaphor of packing a bag to help sort out life's priorities, let us see what it is that we intend to have travel with us into the future. What you put in your hand luggage may be classified as the fragile, the indispensable and the irreplaceable. We pack toiletries, medications, reading material and breakable items in the luggage that will not leave our side.

What do you keep in your heart, on your mind and beneath your smile? Do you carry positive thoughts, an encouraging word, a truthful compliment, inspiring memories with you? What are your precious treasures? Are they photographs of loved ones, the title deed to your home, your certificates, and bank books?

When you travel on to the next life and you have to leave this world, there is nothing that you are allowed to take. You have to send it all ahead of you. How prepared are you to accept that you will one day have to move on? Are you passing your gifts on to others so that the family, or your business, or the ministry you head will continue while you are away, be it on vacation or permanently residing with the Lord? Are your affairs in order? Have you made peace with everyone and are you able to depart in peace? Let God move you to higher heights right here on earth, and plan to travel light.

Tourists

A tourist is a person who is visiting somewhere from another country and intends to return home in a short space of time. We have nearly 5 million people who come to us by air or sea each year. They have left behind the familiar and have ventured into new territory. Most are eager to try new foods, to enjoy local culture, to see historical sights and to talk to some of the people about life in The Bahamas. There is the adventure of water sports, or renting a motor scooter, or driving a car on the "other side of the road."

Very often, tourists want to leave the hotel area and move among neighbourhoods where ordinary people live. Sometimes we have to say a prayer when we see who their guides are as they walk along the streets, and hope that they will not be conned out of anything. A tourist is a vulnerable person who is at the mercy of those who may take advantage of the person's ignorance about location and personalities. It involves placing trust in strangers, while trying to discern who is a friend, and who is not.

We are invited by God to become a tourist in God's world. This means that we come with openness to new situations, we are willing to trust the guides who are sent to us by the Holy Spirit. We have eyes to see and ears to hear all the strange and wonderful happenings that are going on around us.

When we first follow the path that leads to the Kingdom of God, we may indeed come as a spectator. We may come to church and just look at what is going on, but we may not be committed to involvement at any level. If we come as an outsider who has little knowledge of the style of worship to which we are being introduced, we may be very critical or quite overwhelmed. It may take several trips before we can find our way around.

Just as a person who is in a country, where the language is quite foreign, needs an interpreter, so the newcomer to the Kingdom of God will need an interpreter who explains the meaning behind the roles and rituals. It is so helpful to have a spiritual guide who remains with us for the trip and teaches us how to become acclimatized.

Why not approach the life of prayer as a tourist and be willing to attempt new ways of experiencing God? There is 'journaling' which is to write down one's prayers or meditation on a phrase or sentence, such as "we are more than conquerors", to seek revelation on the depth of its meaning. There is the silent contemplation of an object such as the cross, a shell, or a flower allowing oneself to be drawn to new levels of connectedness or understanding. There is praying out loud if you do not usually do so, or to sing your thoughts in your own created songs. There is concert prayer when many pray together, or centering prayer, when one sits in perfect silence to be emptied of all mental busyness.

Come as a tourist into your own home and see if the signs of your faith are visible, or may be experienced within your family. Then make up your mind to apply for citizenship and ask the King to take you from tourist to tithe payer and take up permanent residence around God's throne.

Destinations

Where are some of the places to which you have travelled, if you have been willing to go far away from home? My mother was from Bermuda, two of my grandparents were Jamaican, we had family in the United States and good friends in Canada as well. All these were my earliest destinations as we travelled to secure family ties. It is often a great experience to live with loved ones if they also have children of their own.

Those of us who went to school or college abroad have other places to add to the list. The opportunity to travel at an early age, and live in a different culture during formative years, offers many blessings in disguise. The changes in the weather are a most obvious difference, and can elicit great protest from those of us who do not easily tolerate desert heat or arctic cold. It is helpful, however, to learn to be flexible and to adapt.

There are school trips to practice a foreign language, or job training that requires a time of study abroad. Some relocate to work elsewhere and are tempted never to return home, just as we have been blessed over the years by gifted persons who have worked on our shores. There are exotic places that we learned in geography class that beckon us to come abroad: the various wonders of the world, from Alaska to the Grand Canyon, Africa and Asia, Europe and South America, from Australia to the islands of the Caribbean, there is a great big wonderful world out there waiting to be explored.

Where would you like to see before you die? Are you in a position to start to save a little every day? There are travel discounts on the Internet which offer excellent discounts such as $440 to Hawaii round trip. Travelling with a group can be really good fun if you don't like to go too far alone.

In one sense, death is our final destination as we arrive at the end of this life. This means that our journey is so very important. How you enjoy the days en route, the camaraderie you develop with fellow travellers, the delights you sample, will shape you into the person that determines how you respond to your destination.

We are really in-transit passengers when we pass through death's door if we want to be where God is as our final destination. God wants every one of us to be at home in heaven and heaven is wherever God is. This is how you are able to have a taste of heaven while still on earth. With the coming of Jesus Christ, we are able to experience our final destination even as we travel on the journey, which is a paradox to say the least.

If to be with the Lord is our final destination, let us meet Him in prayer, draw near to Him in praise, and connect with His Spirit in each other.

Family Islands

Let us reflect on the freedom we experience when we leave Nassau to go to a Family Island. How delightful it is to go walking at midnight with no concern at all about crime. Where else can we go wandering in the bushes to catch crabs armed with a flashlight? Some settlements are starting to change, and so we have to do everything in our power to preserve the security that they have been able to maintain.

The runway in Rum Cay has been improved so more of us will be able to discover how warm and friendly those people are. The boat ride to Long Cay through the mangrove swamps is like entering another world, and all those goats on the loose can satisfy the mutton lovers' every fantasy. The salt hills of Inagua, the fish trapped in the pump, the beautiful flamingoes in flight, all make it worthwhile to take a trip down to the far south.

Eleuthera with the contrast of the ocean and the sea, the hills of Gregory Town and quaint towns like Tarpum Bay are a good choice for a week or even a day. The straw work in Red Bays, Andros, the bone fishing in Bimini, yachting in the Exumas, boating in the Berry's, historical sites of San Salvador and Cat Island, these are just some of the reasons to take in every one of our Family Islands. Yes, we are free to explore the countries of the world and there is much to see far and wide, but let us also explore our own islands and be able to speak of them with pride.

God has blessed us with such wealth: white sandy beaches, our emerald seas, gracious people, lovely sites, and sweet ocean breezes. Make it your dream to visit every island in our Bahamas and to take our children too. This is our heritage, this is our Bahamas, and we need to make ourselves more at home in our own home. Let us stop shopping abroad every time we have the chance; let us invest in building up the businesses across the length and breadth of our land.

Why should the tourists enjoy that which God has given to us for free? Why not rent a house with another family, exchange homes with an island friend, or visit some relatives for a few days even if you have to rough it? It will make you appreciate what you have at home, and introduce you to the simplicity of some of our island ways. Go back to your roots, or try somewhere new. The point is to take it all in. We are so blessed with this beautiful land it would be a shame to miss even one of God's gifts to us.

Long Journeys

Abraham had to leave Haran to find his Promised Land. Joseph went to Egypt against his will, but God used his journey to save his family from the famine and to save the Egyptians as well. Moses travelled with the Hebrew slaves through the Red Sea in order to escape oppression from slavery, Naaman had to go to be healed in the River Jordan, and David travelled for years to escape Saul. There is so much movement in the Bible, and it is a theme that is meant to speak to us all.

We are pilgrims on a journey following the promptings of God. Mary and Joseph went to Bethlehem and then to Egypt to fulfill ancient prophecies about the Messiah because of the danger to the Christ child. The wise men followed the star to discover the greatest King of all time. The shepherds left their hills to come to the town. The Lord walked to preach, heal, and teach to bring this peace on earth of which the angels had sung.

The disciples went on missionary journeys to spread the word. Some left because of persecution, but others went to plant churches, re-visit them to encourage the congregations and to assist them to remain strong. Many have followed in their footsteps, and brought the gospel to Spain, England, and the United States of America and to us.

To undertake so many journeys for so many years, these pilgrims were people with a passionate message about the Kingdom of God. How are we making a difference in our generation?

Are we also on the move for God? Are we willing to go wherever we are sent? Will we be as faithful as those who have gone before?

We are also pilgrims on a journey reaching out to others along the way. There is no time to pitch our tent as if we are able to stay. We are on a journey to spread the Good News and we are on an inner journey to find peace within. There are new levels of understanding, new depths of revelation, new experiences of God's presence waiting for us in our own private lives, even as we journey where we are sent.

Life is one long journey, with so much to learn. Faith is another journey as we speak to different groups, counsel individuals and share the gospel with our visitors, who have journeyed to us. When it comes to accepting spiritual truths and living them out in our lives, it has been said that by far the longest journey is from the head to the heart.

YOUR REFLECTIONS

Chapter Four
EXCERPTS FROM THE PAST

Gestures of Love

If we consider the beauty of nature, the gift of human relationships, and the greatest gift of all, the death and resurrection of Jesus Christ, as just some of the ways that God extends love towards us, a heart-felt response should be forthright and forthcoming. We sometimes become so sophisticated, so disillusioned or preoccupied with surviving on our own strength, that we lose the ability to show God any kind of meaningful *gesture of love* at all. Or we may be so caught up with the "otherness," the seeming abstractions of a relationship with One who is unseen, that we are mystified by the concept of loving "from a distance." What is a fitting response?

As with any human relationship, the words "I love you" are a good place to begin. The praise and worship of God is the giving of full attention to *who God is*, and often brings the sweet reward of sensing that one is in the presence of The Almighty. We do not worship in order to feel these feelings. However, we worship because God is worthy of our highest praise, and most deserving of our deepest devotion. We often speak of not being able to thank our human parents enough for all that they have done for us; if we magnify this respect to the point of actual awe and wonder, we will have begun to approach a fitting attitude towards our God.

A thankful heart overflowing with gratitude *for what God has done*, usually brings us to a point of desperately wanting to find suitable ways to respond. Like the woman with the precious ointment, we want to show appreciation for what has been done for us.

We want to give all that we have and are, and hope to be, to a God who loves us beyond imagination. The study of Holy Scripture shows us that Jesus Christ is *'God with us'*, and He bridges the gap.

Why Does Life Have To Hurt So Much?
(From my first publication *"A Medley of Meditations")*

This was a question put by a teenager to an adult. Why? Why do some people suffer, it would appear, so much more than others? Why are we born into handicapping environments that produce spiritual disabilities along with the mental and physical abilities that can be inherited or developed? Is there nothing to anesthetize the pain?

We try to drown our sorrows in drink but this only produces a vicious cycle of addiction and further defeat. We try to ignore our distress by working so hard, and for so long that we are distracted for much of the day. Sometimes, we fall into a death-like sleep, exhausted by the taxing demands being made on the human body, mind and spirit; at other times, we cannot sleep at all.

Frequently, we try to attack the apparent sources of suffering by lashing out at people who cross our war-path, or we wound ourselves further by believing that we have brought it all on ourselves and deserve our suffering. We may even divorce ourselves from all relationships requiring commitment so as never to be hurt again by trusting another fallible soul.

We speak with bitterness and cynicism about the supposedly loving God who is too far away to hear or care. Then we remember the cross, that scandalous event that still defies understanding.

The God of love who cries for us and dies for us, now supplies for us some assurances:

1. There is such a thing as sin.
2. There is such a thing as an evil influence that seeks to spoil God's plan.
3. There is a first person of the Trinity who has the master plan.
4. There is the second person of the Trinity who has salvaged and thwarted the destruction of the plan.
5. There is the third person of the Trinity who is the comforting presence, the compassionate friend, the agent of transformation, healing, growth and change.
6. There are wounded healers who act as coaches along the way to encourage us to persevere, to trust and to obey.

These are mysteries which will be explained in full when the appointed time comes. In the meantime, we look at Jesus, and He lights our path. We see His life of love and joy, His work of reconciliation and redemption. We hear the call to walk in faith and help others along the way.

Like the oyster with the dirt in its shell, we also serve the Lord when we give our grief to Him. Then, in time, the pearly substance will appear, representing the peace of God's presence and power at work, for until one day, we awaken to find the pain gone, and we realize that, finally, we have come through the storm. The heaviness has passed, a new joy in its place, and we find ourselves strengthened by God's amazing grace. When life hurts, let God heal.

Death, Where Is Thy Sting?
(From *"Seasons of the Church"*)

If we turn to the obituary column we will see that every day death continues to steal persons of all ages and stages of life. It is obvious then, that one of the ministries of the church needs to be the ongoing preparation of its people for the inevitable.

As we seek to prepare ourselves for our own deaths, let us look at what God has promised to Christians in the words of Holy scripture: God is with us always even to the end of the world (Mt. 28:20). Nothing can separate us from the love of God in Christ Jesus...Not even death (Rom. 8:35-39); Jesus has gone to prepare a place for us (John. 14: 2-3).

Sometimes it is helpful to use an image like that of the caterpillar and the butterfly to capture the spirit of the transforming power of death in Christ. In this context, resurrection means leaving the cocoon of the grave to fly into eternity. Thus, whether we live in Christ or die in Christ, as long as we are in Christ, it really does not matter.

To grieve for a loved one is human; to grieve with hope is Christian. We are called to place our trust in the good God who has loved us all for our lives and has been faithful to us from the beginning. God will help us to bear even this temporary separation.

In our attempts to comfort the bereaved, let us remember two things:

- The silent presence of one who enters our suffering and mourns with us can often do more than many well-meaning words.
- In the very early stages of grief before doing things becomes therapeutic, practical assistance by thoughtful friends can ease the burdens of the daily routines and rituals (meals, laundry, baby-sitting, and transportation).

If we live each day for the Lord, as if it were indeed our last, then we need have no regrets when our time comes. Let us look at this world and see its beauty each day. Let us look at our loved ones and cherish their presence as blessings from God. Let us accept ourselves with humble dignity, seeking to please God first and foremost, in all that we say and do. Then, when our time does come, having lived each day to the fullest, in the knowledge that even better days lie ahead in eternal life, we can meet death face to face, and echo Apostle Paul's famous words: "Death, where is thy sting?" (1 Cor. 15:55)

Adolescents
(From the cassette tape entitled "Praying With and for Children")

Who am I? Where am I going? Why was I created? Is there anything special about me? These are just some of the questions that plague our young people at this time of transition. No longer a little child and not really an adult, these are often difficult years in which there is a real need for an anchor to keep them from being swept away.

Our prayers for them will greatly influence our attitude toward them. If we pray for them to learn to settle quietly and listen to God's voice deep within, we may find it easier to trust the decisions they try to make based on what they think they have discerned.

Our offer of prayerful support says to them that we know that we are not their Lord and master, only senior travellers who care for them as we all journey across the mysterious road of life. In humility and love, we seek to guide and direct their paths with the instructions we have diligently sought from the Lord. They need to know that we are not in charge of our own affairs either, but are trying to be a child before God, while being an adult to the world.

One of the greatest gifts is to teach them how to listen to the Lord. The ability to be still before God and wait in prayerful silence for the Lord, or a word from the Lord, is the most blessed of spiritual experiences.

From an early age, some children are aware of the voice of conscience, or the whisper of God telling them right from wrong. They may choose to ignore it, but most have heard an inner prompting, I believe.

This inner communication is just one of the ways that God speaks to us, and a listening ear should be cultivated as soon as possible.

At other times, a word from the Lord comes while reading scripture when God allows a word or phrase to remain on our hearts. It is our responsibility to teach them to pray as they read, and to study a bible with a modern translation and with foot-notes to assist with the internalizing of the word which can then be brought back to their remembrance at a later time.

Praying with music has a great appeal for many people. Quiet worship songs and the more up-beat praise choruses keep the mind focused, and the spirit dances before the Lord, even as the body may do so as well. Encourage adolescents to write their own psalms, prayers and songs in which they capture their faith experience. One day they may be published, or just passed on within the family, or retained as a part of the prayer journal method.

The Psalms are so emotional that many young people will easily identify with the need to express pain and to protest. When feelings are hard to articulate or adults refuse to listen, writing offers both relief and release. By reading the Psalms and writing our own, many of us are helped to survive the storms of suffering, and go on to thrive in ministry to the honour and glory of God.

Entering God's Presence
(The first prayer cassette)
This is a simple breathing exercise to relax the body, focus the mind and enable the spirit to be open to the Holy Spirit's movement.

Exercise 1

First, become aware of the rhythm of your normal breath flow. Try not to alter the pace. Recognize the work that takes place as a reflex action both day and night. Thank God for the wonder of who you are.

Gently hold the breath for as long as is comfortable, exhaling when ready. As you do this several times, reflect on the cleansing and nourishing aspects of oxygen which flows through the bloodstream to every cell of your body. Note the release of carbon dioxide with each exhalation to remove certain impurities from the system.

As you continue to control your breathing, imagine that as you breathe in, you are being filled with the very breath of God. Just as God breathed into Adam in one of the Genesis accounts of creation, and as God also breathed into the bodies in the valley of dry bones in Ezekiel's vision in chapter 37.

As you return to a more natural breathing rhythm, allow yourself to notice that the quieter steady flow is like your spirit praying on your behalf without your mind having to dictate. While you breathe you can pray. May "praying without ceasing", in the words of St. Paul, become your secret joy as you journey with the Lord!

Exercise 2.

Our second exercise also uses the breath but this time we will focus on your inner feelings. What is your strongest feeling at the moment? You may have mixed feelings such as anger and sadness, or fear and anxiety, or joy and sadness, depending on the circumstances.

As you exhale, release one of those feelings to God and pray to be filled with the quality of Christ, or the fruit of the Holy Spirit, which corresponds. For example, you may be feeling frightened and need to be filled with God's peace, or feeling unloved and need to be filled with a sense of God's overwhelming love for you.

Guilt and shame may be released as a form of sincere confession, as you acknowledge the situation before God. You acknowledge God's forgiveness, and empowering to help you. Remember, every day, while you breathe, you can pray.

YOUR REFLECTIONS

Chapter Five
FOLLOWING GOD'S LEAD

Following God's Lead

In the well-known story of the Hebrews in the desert, we find the prophet Nehemiah recounting: "You in your great mercies did not forsake them in the wilderness; the pillar of cloud that led them in the way did not leave them by day, nor the pillar of fire by night that gave them light or the way by which they should go" (Nehemiah 9:19). The idea was to have something so visible to every person in the crowd that they would not be able to doubt that God was with them, and they would follow the path that had been chosen for them. What are the pillars of clouds and pillars of fire in our lives? How do we know that we are on the right path? How can we feel sure that God is with us?

Most of us had someone, and still have some special people, who pray with and for us, offering godly counsel from time to time. They may be living out their truth to such a degree that we admire them for their consistency. For example, a financial advisor who is doing well by following the same guidelines given is far more credible than someone who is not taking the same risks, or using the same principles, or one who is almost bankrupt. Even the best guide is fallible, so we need to look for an infallible one.

Books written over the years that have become classics are another great source of enlightenment. There are timeless spiritual aids written by the famous and the obscure, along with hymns and folk songs that highlight various truths.

When you are in the desert, stripped down to the lightest possible load that you may have to carry for forty years, it is quite a different story. It helps to be with a group travelling in the same direction to keep your company, help you with the burdens and offer encouragement. It is wonderful to have spiritual leaders who are obedient enough to part the Red Sea and intercede on your behalf. It is still necessary to keep your own eye on the pillar of cloud and the pillar of fire from time to time. You do not want to just follow any crowd and anywhere.

Your prayer life allows God to reveal to you the signs of your own times. As you settle and become still, your own thoughts will part like the Red Sea and your spirit will walk through to the other side, where you will find the answers you need. Certain scriptures will come to your remembrance, if you read your Bible daily, and allow them to become recorded permanently in your memory bank. Your participation in regular workshop and fellowship opportunities exposes you to the wisdom and teaching of others, to their experiences and hopeful expectations. Your faithful and enthusiastic service will bless you with the lessons only to be learnt from giving and loving selflessly, with no desire for reciprocation or favour being returned.

You want to stay with the crowd when you lose sight of the pillars for brief periods of time, but do not become so dependent on others that you neglect your ability to see and believe for yourself. God wants to be seen and heard in your everyday life in quiet ways. God wants you to follow the path of loving obedience. You will not be forsaken, no matter how vast or distressing your wilderness. God will be your oasis in the desert, and keep you fed and watered all along the way.

The Wilderness

"Can God set a table in the wilderness?" is the question voiced by the Hebrews as deliberated in Psalm 78. We may wonder why they are so faithless, but is it possible that we too may be guilty of the same crime?

What are some of the modern day wildernesses that we face? Are there not times when we hear, watch or read the news, and we think that surely evil is taking over the world and that we are helpless to resist? Think of the situation in the Sudan, refugees in crowded slums, illegal immigrants fleeing political or economic chaos or just looking for a better way of life. The damage to the ozone layer and the tremendous heat we experience in summer comes as a result of the "greenhouse effect". Incest, indiscriminate abortion, sexual promiscuity, domestic violence, crime and corruption, there is no end to the many wildernesses that may come to mind when we look around us today.

"Can God set a table in the wilderness?" You bet. This is the same God, who "Prepares a table before me in the presence of my enemy," (Psalm 23). Sometimes it takes hard times to get God's people to sit down at the table in the first place. What is it that God wants to set on our table today?

First of all, be still for a moment and think about the kind of wilderness you are in. Are there enemies? Are there dangers? Is it a peaceful place to withdraw to in order to pray? Did you choose to be in this wilderness? Did someone exile you to this place? How long have you been wandering in it? Is it because you refuse to follow the pillars of cloud and light, the signs of God's plan for your direction that you are still in this wilderness? What do you think you need God to do for you to get you out? Are you alone or are there some other people sharing your experience?

If you are alone, it may be that you don't need to be, and God may be directing you to find those of like mind and journey together. If it is sin keeping you in, then you know the way out. If you don't know what is going on, see if you can find some guidelines from the Lord regarding your very next step.

We all have wilderness moments, but God is always setting up some table or other. We have more power than we realize if we join together to combat various social ills, do preventive education, offer supportive companionship, and work to legislate change approaches. Start by yourself if you have to, but try to invite a few others in. While I put a blessing on your table, God may use you to put a blessing on mine. God is a supplier of needs. You may be the source of the supply. Whom you least expect may be sent as the source for your supply.

Trust God, seek God, surrender to God, and enjoy what God has to offer. With the right company, good food, and a satisfied spirit, you may even forget that you are in your wilderness.

The Impossible Separation

Sometimes we cannot forget the wilderness that we are in because we cannot even eat. We are so broken we do not even see the table set before us: eyes swollen shut with weeping, heart heavy and spirit crushed. We are oblivious to any comfort or consolation. Desolate, despairing, despondent and dejected, we feel as if we will bleed to death, while others just pass by on the other side.

Romans 8:35-39 was given to us as a gift for such a time as this: *"Who will separate us from the love of Christ? Will hardship, or distress, or persecution, or famine, or nakedness, or peril, or sword? As it is written, 'For your sake we are being killed all day long; we are accounted as sheep to be slaughtered.' No, in all these things we are more than conquerors through him, who loved us. For I am convinced that neither death, nor life, nor angels, nor rulers, nor things present, nor things to come, nor powers, nor height, nor depth, nor anything else in all creation, will be able to separate us from the love of God in Christ Jesus our Lord."*

Are you permitting someone to separate you from the love of Christ? You need to take the initiative for yourself to establish, or re-establish your priorities and ask God to separate you from the influence or power of this person. Then remember you are always free to pray and talk to God in the secret place of your own heart.

What is the nature of your hardship? What is the extent of your distress? Why are you suffering persecution and in what form? What are you starving for in your time of famine? Of what have you been stripped in your time of nakedness? How great is your peril? Who is holding the sword?

No matter what your individual answer, St. Paul is convinced that you will be more than a conqueror through the One who loved us enough to die on the cross. When you open yourself to a saving faith, you too will become convinced that you do not have to be afraid of dying. You will not be separated from Christ in death as a result of the reality of the resurrection. There is nothing in life that need separate us because no matter the circumstance, we are free to abide in Jesus if we invite Him to abide in us. The angels are under his authority, rulers on earth need not be permitted to weaken our faith as Daniel modelled for us in the lions' den.

There is nothing in our present situation, nothing in the future, and nothing in our past that can separate us from God if we do not desire it to be so. Not even the powers of Satan or any other evil spirits, demons, imps, principalities of any kind are strong enough to sever the bonds of love that Christ has for us. Nothing in the heights, down in the depths or anything, anywhere in creation, has the power to cancel out the price Christ paid.

So what are we waiting for? Let us explore all the blessings such a relationship has to offer.

Let us do nothing to separate ourselves from the best friend we will ever have. We most certainly need the ongoing and sustaining love of Christ embodied in the Holy Spirit's presence.

We have the pillar of cloud and the pillar of fire on the inside of us. 'The cloud of unknowing' as one author calls it, and the fire of enlightenment that Pentecost introduced. We are ready for anything God requires of us. We are not alone and we are not helpless with Christ on our side.

The Feeding

What kind of God do we have that orchestrates this kind of evening outdoor picnic that can feed five thousand? Many of them had been cured of sickness Matthew tells us in Chapter 14. They were so elated that they may not have noticed that they were hungry.

The disciples are no doubt hungry themselves, and so they realize that the crowd is hungry too. They come and make representation with a very practical suggestion. It keeps the responsibility away from them and places it on the people who can go into the surrounding villages and buy food for themselves.

The Lord has a better idea. He decides to let the disciples become more intimately involved. This is ministry at its best. We see the need, we come to Jesus with what we have, and Jesus meets the needs of numbers beyond measure. Jesus prays, blesses and breaks the loaves for the disciples to distribute.

How could they or we miss the point that the deserted place does not dictate the supply? The desert has hidden resources. The crowd has resources to contribute. We are all in this together. The time, the place, nor the 'magnitude of the multitude' determines how God's love will operate.

This is their manna in the wilderness and, instead of quail, this time it is fish. The table is set before them as it were, with enough food to satisfy, and some astounded but obedient servants to serve it. That was quite a number to feed and pick up after. If it can be this good in the wilderness, what must it be like on fertile ground, in the Promised Land or at the heavenly banquet?

If you are in the crowd at the moment, eat and be satisfied with what God provides for you. If your situation is desperate, then some servants should be near with some supplies. If you are a disciple, then your part is to be with the people for as long as it takes for them to hear what Jesus is trying to say. Be practical even as you are concerned with spiritual needs.

Drive your message home with hands-on ministry. All who are leaders, clergy or lay people, are to be involved in blessing those in need. Accept the offerings of those willing to give and then share them around equally. Do not be overwhelmed by the numbers in the wilderness, or the seemingly limited resources. Be satisfied with the bare essentials, follow God's lead, assess the nature of the wilderness, reject any thought of separation from Christ for any reason, and then get on with feeding as many thousands that need to be strengthened in body, mind and spirit. As you feast on the love with which they are being fed, you too will find yourself truly satisfied.

Faith & Fear

Suppose you accept a position or a challenge and you find that the conditions are more intimidating than you anticipated. What if you become aware of limitations previously undetected? What will you do? Are you easily discouraged? Do you bend in the face of opposition without a struggle?

It helps to feel that you are capable and equipped. It helps to find doors opening and opportunities presenting themselves daily. Like a good drop when you are out fishing, every hook that is baited brings up a catch. Sometimes it is like this. Every thing you touch turns to gold, though it is not always the case. Very often it only takes one supportive family member or friend who really believes in you and shares your dream to help you remain focused on the end of the road.

If it is a wise plan and you are convinced that it is from the Lord, then distractions weaken your faith and instill a spirit of fear, if you are not well anchored to the rock of God's will for your life. Like wilks or barnacles which cling so tenaciously to the rocks, we have to cling to our convictions that what God asks is possible.

Think of Peter who asks Jesus to allow him to walk on the stormy waves of the Sea of Galilee, as Jesus is doing. He starts out doing very well while he is directing his attention to the one who has called him out of the boat. As soon as he allows himself to become preoccupied with the winds and the waves, he starts to sink.

This story has a lesson for all of us to learn. Fear will threaten to overwhelm us when we realize how out numbered we are by enemies or how inadequate we are to maintain a sustained level of productivity. The key is to recognize that we will have times of weakness and distress. We were never intended to live our lives without the help of God. At some point we get "cold feet" and find ourselves sinking. Do not allow yourself to be drowned by the cares of this world, the fears of your mind, or the sneers or your critics. Since God is for you, you will be strengthened to accomplish what has been required of you.

Determine whether or not you are in God's will before you get out of the boat. Once you start to do what only God can enable you to do, stay present to the power of God in prayer and by the reading of scriptural material. Remember that if you start to sink, you can call for help. Even if you find yourself under the waves for one reason or another you have a strong deliverer.

The best way to stay above the waves is keep praising and thanking God. Nothing will separate you from God's power and purpose to save and deliver us. Do not be afraid, only believe.

YOUR REFLECTIONS

PART II

STAYING ATTACHED TO THE VINE AS A PEOPLE

Chapter Six
WISDOM FROM THE WORD

King David

Psalm 119:129-136 are a few verses in a very long Psalm that celebrates the wisdom to be found in God's laws. These laws are found mainly in the Old Testament. If we think of God's laws as rules, principles, guidelines or commandments, we see that we are talking about a structure for our lives. There are boundaries and limits which are set and are explained by the Lord to help us celebrate our freedom within restrictions. When we put a fence or wall around our property, it gives us added protection, security and privileges in our designated area.

We usually follow traffic signals without thinking about their real significance. Not until someone violates our reasonable expectations and runs a light or drives towards us in our lane, do we understand just how important it is for traffic laws to be followed and enforced. Headlights that do not work and turning signals that are not used make driving so much more dangerous. Pedestrians will vouch for the precarious position that they are in when speeding motorists refuse to stop at pedestrian crossings.

Laws that have to do with our health or our wealth, laws that govern the judicial system or national safety are no different from moral laws and spiritual laws that need to be applied.

The consequences of breaking any law, if consistently enforced, may be avoided merely by complying with the law. There is no point in testing the truth about the force of gravity using a new chandelier. If it is not properly secured, it will fall and shatter.

Why is it that we insist on flouting God's laws about sexual behaviour or respect for persons and property, and not expect to have time-proven consequences follow? Perhaps the shattering of our spiritual treasures is not as immediately noticeable, but the loss is even more devastating if we could measure their worth and value.

When we have wisdom and discernment, such as King Solomon asked for, we are able to move our existence to a new level. We begin to think more of God's thoughts as truth revealed to us in scripture. Like the Psalmist we can say: "Your decrees are wonderful; therefore my soul keeps them. The unfolding of your words gives light; it imparts understanding to the simple." Our steps are kept steady and we are rescued from oppression.

We weep when we read or see violations occurring, and we are often moved to act to fight against injustice in ways that please God. Which of God's laws do you break too easily? How can you experience more of God's face shining upon you? Read Psalm 119 for yourself and receive wisdom.

In 1 Kings 3:5, God appears to Solomon in a dream and tells him: "Ask what I should give you." Solomon answers: "Give your servant therefore an understanding mind to govern your people, able to discern between good and evil." What would your reaction be if God gave you the choice to ask for whatever you wanted? Would it be things, or even for yourself? Would you ask for healing for a spouse or parent, or a job for your child? Would it be for the nation or the world?

In this case, Solomon is aware that at his young age and lacking experience, he needs God's help to be a good king. God is so pleased with Solomon's answer since it does not involve long life, or riches or the life of his enemies that not only is he given the wisdom he desires, but the riches and honour as well. When you come to think of it we all need to begin with wisdom and discernment to choose right from wrong.

Even little children need discernment to withstand peer pressure and adult advances, much less our youth and young adults. Whether single or married, employee or boss, unemployed or underemployed, there are many key decisions to be made. Leaders and followers, parents and grandparents, persons in every trade or profession need to make right choices every minute.

Clergy especially need your prayers for wisdom to be applied to our personal lives, our preaching, teaching, counselling and pastoral care. All of us then, need wisdom to govern ourselves, the upcoming generations and persons we influence. Every christian certainly needs wisdom to please God.

If you pause for a moment and anticipate what you have planned, or with what you normally have to deal, for what do you need wisdom today? Then factor in the unexpected that will take you quite off guard. You know that you will not want to face this day all on your own, in your own strength or drawing on your own limited understanding.

From the gift of wisdom will come patience for example, because you will better discern the dynamics of a situation and be more prepared to trust the Lord. Your inner peace will more than likely increase as you improve your health with better eating schedules and selections, necessary exercise, rest and water consumption, handling your relationships with less irritability and anger.

Your joy will multiply as you see how God will use you to make disciples through your developing love for others, and modelling of spiritual maturity in the form of a strong faith and powerful testimony.

You do not have to wait for God to come to you in a dream. Just ask for the Holy Spirit to give you wisdom and discernment right now. It is yours for the asking.

Saint Paul

In Romans 8:26-34, the Apostle Paul reminds us that often our ignorance and inadequacy so overwhelms us that we are unable to get free from the chains that bind us. Just like the dove who would have yearned for freedom but would have found no safe way to escape, we realize that we are in no position to liberate ourselves from our weaknesses and failings. Sometimes we are so caught in the snare that we do not even know what is wrong with us and what we need to set us free.

This is where the good news of the gospel comes in. If this is how you are feeling, then it will be a relief for you to know that God does not expect you to find your own way out of your present mess. In fact, the Holy Spirit is available to you to help you in your weakness because you do not even know how to pray sometimes. This is why the Spirit of God intercedes for us "with sighs too deep for words". The Holy Spirit discerns the will of God for our lives and prays it for us, and soon we begin to long for the very things that God wants to give us.

With Jesus Christ as our Saviour who intercedes for us in heaven, and the Holy Spirit within us teaching us how to pray, how to wait upon the Lord, how to recognize the good that God can bring out of every situation, what more do we need? We come to appreciate the way God works, those divine operating principles or spiritual laws and we come to know for ourselves "that all things work together for good for those who love God, who are called according to his purpose" (v. 28).

God wants every one of us to be set free from the bondage

of sin, from the feeling that 'I just can't do anything right without messing up somehow and hurting myself, or someone else or both'.

It is such a struggle, and even when you get on the "good foot" there are those guilty memories and nagging doubts that want to suck you back down into old ways of thinking or being. Those "flesh pots of Egypt" keep threatening to overwhelm the children of liberated Hebrew slaves, so that they are tempted to forsake the journey towards the Promised Land and go back under Pharaoh's rule.

There is no turning back now for us as a people, or for you as an individual. Greater is the One within you than any that can come against you and nothing you have done in the past has power to chain you or enslave you, if you keep asking the Holy Spirit for the wisdom to keep you free. Keep praying and trusting God. The Lord did not bring you this far to leave you now.

Saint Matthew

The difficulty about seeing the Promised Land as an emancipated sinner is that it is so subtle at first. The Kingdom of Heaven or the Promised Land came with Jesus Christ, but it is hidden from those who do not have spiritual wisdom. When Jesus Christ becomes king of your life you automatically become a citizen of the kingdom. The kingdom is in you and you are in the kingdom, if Jesus Christ lives in you and you live in Him.

St. Matthew's Gospel 13:31-33, 44-49a tell us what to expect from this kingdom living in several examples that are taken from ordinary Jewish life at the time. He tells of seed, yeast, treasure, pearls and nets of fish. Bear in mind that if the kingdom is in us, we have the seed, yeast, treasure, pearl, and power to sort good and evil, right inside of us.

A mustard seed was the tiniest of seeds but when planted became a huge tree that birds could nest in. The kingdom starts out small and hidden in you, or in a situation where you "plant" God's will, but the results will soon be very obvious, very beneficial and so much more than its simple beginning. The yeast is also hidden, and looks so unassuming until it is mixed into the flour and the results are amazingly abundant, a mystifying increase, unless you understand the process.

The treasure that is hidden is first found, and then hidden again, until the field can be bought so that the treasure belongs to the new owner, who appreciates its worth and value to such a degree that everything else is joyfully sold to purchase it. So it is with the buyer of pearls. He was convinced that he had the best deal in town.

What is it that could possibly mean this much? Have you found it yet? I believe that it is a sense of God's love for me that makes me want to give everything I am back to God. God wants me to work for the kingdom, and is pleased when I do. God wants me to become more like Jesus, letting the selfish me decrease and be filled like an overflowing fountain with the joy, peace, love, faith, hope and other qualities of Christ. God wants the same for you.

What about you? Do you want to be the seed that disappears and then emerges as a sheltering tree? Do you want to work the yeast of ministry into the flour of the Church and see God do amazing things with your effort? Do you know what is worth having that is better than anything else?

It takes wisdom to know just how free you really can be to have all that God wants for you. Don't let Satan keep you in bondage. Let Jesus set you free.

YOUR REFLECTIONS

CHAPTER SEVEN
JUNKANOO

Dreaming

I remember some years when the fringing was long and shaggy, with newspaper being used by some individuals determined to get on the street. Now the costumes have evolved into exquisitely delicate masterpieces of kaleidoscopic colours, with feathers and jewels, flashing lights and glitter.

Who are the dreamers? Who are the creative artists who see the theme in their mind's eye and sell the vision to the group, not for a price, but for passionate approval? Over the years, it seems as if we have seen every imaginable combination of things, old and new, and yet there is always something different. The size of the crowds, the installation of increasing numbers of bleachers, and the rave reviews are a clear indication that the lure of the mesmerizing magic of Junkanoo is stronger than ever.

God's gift of the imagination makes us co-creators so that designs seem to appear out of thin air. This is how we all came to be created. The fertile and holy word was spoken and creation began: "Let there be" and we were. Introduced at the end of the creation narrative, human beings are made to reflect the glory of God, the splendour of royalty in the presence of the King of kings.

The Junkanoo music sends messages to the mind, and it is the handiwork of another dreamer to capture sounds that speak to the spirit. Is it the call of our African ancestors that we hear in the drums? Is it the rhythm of the maternal heartbeat that takes us back into forgotten experiences of the womb? Do we sway like our coconut trees? Is it the surge of the sea?

Perhaps it is the sense of celebration that we seek. We want to feel unencumbered by cares and unrestricted by routine.

When we come into God's sanctuary, we are called to march to the beat of a different drum. We are called to participate in the very act of re-creation. The winning theme is that of the Kingdom of God, where the King is in control. If we permit ourselves to be redesigned by the Master Crafter of all times, what eternal display of magnificence and majesty that will be, when our true self is allowed to be revealed, and the beauty and wonder of who we all are is finally unveiled. It is only a matter of each of us saying, as the Junkanoo members say when they come for their costumes in the shack: "Lord I come to get me."

Designing

Once the themes have been selected, it is now time to begin to design the elaborate costumes which will reproduce the concept into many dimensions. On cardboard, the individual creations begin to take form, and special gifts are brought to bear on this particular task. The accuracy, the symmetry, the invisible beauty has yet to emerge in vibrant living colour, yet even at this point, the untrained eye is able to detect the intricacy of the unfolding tapestry.

In countless shacks all over this island, there are patient artists labouring with love. Who measures the long hours that are willingly spent to make the invisible visible? One step at a time, one day at a time, one piece at a time, work progresses until the whole group portrays blueprints of artistic brilliance. Like dedicated monks who copied out scripture word by word, these hypnotized hermits work to complete their task.

It is interesting to see just how human beings are capable of putting body and soul into something in which they believe.

Determined dedication keeps us with our shoulder to the wheel if we consider the production worth the perspiration.

The Lord laboured to deliver us as a holy people, hungering and thirsting after our righteousness. His self-contained glory modelled meekness for us as he resisted all short cuts to salvation. He mourned over the destruction of God's design for Jerusalem. He was persecuted because he would not conform to established patterns, but insisted that we be transformed to a heavenly plan.

Each of our lives is more elaborately intricate and personally precious to God than the beloved pieces of the Junkanoo costumes. If so much is sacrificed by so many to create fragile forms of transitory beauty, how do we determine their worth? Is there a dollar amount that can do justice to the time, energy, love that goes into the designing of lead pieces and costumes?

You are God's lead piece. You lead creation in a pulsating pageant of spectacle and ceremony. You are intended to leave angels breathless. You are destined for a spiritual greatness that is reserved for the glorious children of God.

Let the Almighty Artist, the Divine Designer, impress on you the mystery of your majesty. Submit, surrender, succumb to the unfolding eternal plan, as if you were cardboard awaiting the touch of the Master's Hand. We cannot see the finished product. We cannot determine how our suffering and salvation, sacrifice and success all blend together within God's divine purpose. We can only trust that love will not lead us anywhere less than toward our blessed best. Let the Designer finish your design.

Pasting

Little pieces of mosaic-like fringe, flat rows of "buds", jewels, glitter, feathers and tinsel all add glamour to this seemingly flat design. Following the instructions as outlined, the abstract becomes concrete, the intangible real. The colours slowly begin to appear. Each one works with obedience according to prescribed outlines. There is an individual contest for some pieces, and there is the overall goal of the team: to win. Individually, and collectively, judgments will have to be made. There is a personal pressing towards the mark of one's own success, and a group graciousness that keeps one in tune with the rest of the Junkanoo Family.

Time and effort have to go into each piece; no sloppy work is encouraged. As the judges pass through the ranks, each one wants to contribute to the overall effect of general similarities. Interesting how there is a simultaneous development of a collective consciousness. The group has won together and lost together. The group has had drummers praised one year and dancers criticized, or group organization applauded but costumes condemned. Over the years, there is sensitivity to certain comments, and the acceptance or rejection of certain defeats.

What if we could each see ourselves more as a large Bahamian family with individual personality prizes and a team trophy as well? There is too much at stake to be so overly concerned with our own costume that we selfishly make the rest of the team wait, or we are so busy getting our piece to Bay Street that we are not there to help the others who may otherwise come late.

We are all in this together though we each have our own design. There is a wider picture, a greater good than what is in it for me and mine. God is calling us to take more care of the others in our group. The crimes, the stealing, the adultery and the deceit, have no place here or it spells national defeat.

When will we move beyond our selfishness, our spotlight selling of self? There is a better way to reflect God's glory, and it is God's plan that the rest of the group receive their blessings as well.

We may be a marvellous masterpiece and we are pleased with our own inner worth, but everyone else is as wondrously made and is of equal value to God.

In this great heavenly Junkanoo parade (developing the metaphor further), we are all hoping for the prize, but it is more important to win the group category. Let me see your inner beauty as you reflect the glory of God, and you may marvel at what God has done for me, and together, we will all reach for the stars.

Practising

The time of year will soon be determined by the sound of the horns, bells and drums, as the music section starts to practice with a vengeance. Sweet victory in the year before needs to be maintained, disappointing defeats have to be reversed. There is so much to energize them into action.

A group that practices near to where I lived works late into the evening to perfect their musical pieces. Strong sounds fill the air with urgency and intensity. This is serious business; yet, there is joy and excitement.

Small crowds gather to thrill to the sounds; even the competitors are impressed by that which is really good. Over and over and over again, they rehearse until the good becomes better, and eventually the group is convinced that they are the best. The dancers practice their steps in private until they have them all memorized, and then the 'putting it all together' must begin. Everything has to be perfect on that day. Precision with power, rhythms and routines all have to ebb and flow together.

When we come before the Lord with our music of various kinds, and dance before our God with reverence, this is really living. Draped in our regal robes, some will sway majestically, and others will clap and chant. In the beauty of holiness, all will eventually (we hope), stand before the Lord in worshipping silence, with God in us and around us, and we gaze at that which may be unseen by others, but which leaves us in awe.

We are called to practice the harmony of heaven even while we inhabit the earth. There is the learning of individual lessons to handle our distinctive giftedness, but we also have to keep time with the team. No matter how exotic our dance steps, they are choreographed to reflect the theme. As we practice, we improve, as we improve, we inspire others to do the same.

If you practice your faith first to please God, and to lead others in the dance of righteousness and truth, you will be such an asset to us all. Let your mouth be filled with praise, and your prayers depend on God's promises. Keep the beat of holy living, play the tune of a thankful heart, dance to the glory of God by your loving, so that you help set your whole team on fire. Now invite us in from the side lines to feel the pulse of Christ's blood in your veins, and even the sick and broken hearted will dance in spite of their pain.

Parading

Well, well, well, what a time: All the people out there in their line. The lead pieces with the banner, the dancers, the musicians and everyone else all resplendent in glory, bursting with enthusiasm, adrenalin pumping, they are raring to go; they want to get out in front of those bleachers and put on their well-rehearsed show.

No one has even seen this moment. The theme has taken a life of its own, and the months of hard labour have come to an end. It is now or never. The pieces may have been admired individually, the music has been heard before, and the dance steps are familiar, but no one has experienced the combined effect.

There is hardly time to really admire the sea of colour and sound; the video is probably the only way for the participants to see what makes the crowds soar. In a few short hours, it will all be over. History will have been made. Then it will be back to the drawing board for the next year's design to try and keep ahead of the game.

When we line up for that saintly procession with the redeemed in their robes of white, gold, silver jewels, feathers, and whatever else God chooses, we will be a more glorious sight. Perhaps the martyrs will have the lead pieces, the choirs of angels will play in the band, and the little ones who lost their lives will dance before God with delight, on that 'great getting up morning', when the "dead in Christ will arise", and the living are caught up in glory to meet Him in the skies. When all the faithful are countless in number too vast for our eyes, there will be no end to the singing and dancing of this final jubilee.

So let God get your costume ready, the robes of righteousness made from above. Get the instrument of your praising voice in tune to say, "Holy, Holy, Holy," and "We praise you, O God," because this church meeting will never come out. This is the moment we live for when God will wipe those tears from our eyes; no more sinning, no more sorrow, no more dying, no more wickedness to take us by surprise. No spectators on this day, so come participate in the parade of God's plan. Let the blessing of God fall on you this day, be you boy or girl, woman or man.

YOUR REFLECTIONS

Chapter Eight
INDEPENDENCE

Behind Closed Doors

As we think about national issues where there is a need for a change in current trends, and where concerned citizens have to become involved, we return to the subject of what goes on behind closed doors. Where do we begin to work for change?

Let each of us look to our own affairs first, in order to evaluate the beam or the plank which may be in our own eyes, before we try to remove the splinter that is another person's problem, says the Lord.

If you are single, what are your living conditions like? Are you comfortable where you are? How do you spend your money? Are you able to grow spiritually in your current situation? Who do you have to pray with to grow more like Christ and bloom, or wait to be transplanted? Is your present lifestyle a credit to your family, an asset to your nation, and a blessing to the name of the Lord? Do you want to change if it is not, and what is the first step that you need to take today?

If you are married, how are you living out this commitment? How do you handle one another? Will you go for help if it is not healthy? Can you allow yourselves to admit your needs to God and begin to speak the truth in love, be accountable for the sake of the gospel, and model the Christ-like qualities that are expected of christians? If you are not a christian are your values and morals shaping your life so that you may be a positive influence, or are you in need of some foundational principles?

If you are a parent, are you making the needs of your children of high priority? Are you spending enough time to teach them how to be secure in a changing world, by modelling inner peace and a mature approach to problem solving? Are you planning to keep your family small enough to enable each child to have sufficient time with you, and to nurture them and care for them properly? If your life seems out of control, come to some counsellor for help.

Are you a young person who is anxious about the future and overwhelmed by life? Remember that you have the grace of God within you to help you to take just one day at a time, and handle it to the best of your ability. Rely on the guidance of God's inner voice reminding you of what is right and what is wrong. Look for adults who are living decent and upright lives, and emulate them.

Once you can open your closed doors, you may invite others to visit with you as you share together hard truths. You may knock on other closed doors with the light of Christ to help them brighten their surroundings and find hope. We who are leaders in every sphere have to lead in spiritual and moral matter first of all.

Our National Institutions

There are those who do not live behind a door that closes or a single-family dwelling. There are some of us who live together in larger units.

What is it like to be in an orphanage? How do we support the Ranfurly Home for Children and other children's homes? Who will buy the dining room chairs needed or repair the broken back wall? Will you help the repairs get done at these homes? Are you willing to call any one of them and ask what you can do to help?

What about the homes for the elderly? Have you visited any? Is there any way that you can use your gifts to be a blessing to a senior person? Can you spare one hour a week or even a month to love someone outside of your immediate circle?

What about our medical institutions? Are you willing to make helpful donations after you enquire what different wards may need or clinics may use? Are you honest with your dealings so that you do not rob or abuse the system? Are you praying for creative ways to encourage the hard-working members of staff?

Our penal institutions house those who have deviated from the norm, or are accused of doing so. How can we redirect a path, soften a hard heart, or work for change in some way? How can their tremendous amounts of time be used, their energy channelled, and their creativity developed to enhance our nation even behind bars? What kind of life skills can be taught, and spiritual and educational progress made for them to be in a position to compensate the victims of their crimes?

What about our educational system? How do we help an overburdened system to ensure that every graduate is capable of reading, writing and comprehension at an acceptable level? Are we willing to offer our time or to help pay for more remedial staff persons, guidance counsellors, social workers, chaplains and others who are trained to assist those in need? How seriously do you want to bring change? What are you willing to sacrifice to do so? We may not think that we have extra time or extra money or extra energy, but we have to sacrifice in order to do our share.

This is no time to think of ourselves only. We have to see that divided we fall. While it is day, let us work. While we have strength, let us contribute. While we have breath, let us pray. Our help is in the Lord who has made heaven and earth, and our hope is in the plan God has for us as a people.

The Bare Essentials

If I were to ask you to describe what you need to survive, with only the bare essentials, what would you say? If the world did go into major economic recession what could you do without and still be happy? Perhaps if we begin to emotionally distance ourselves from the non-essentials, we will appreciate them while we have them, but feel no anxiety if we have to give them up.

When the electrical company had to move a pole near our home, it was done in the late evening so as not to inconvenience the surrounding businesses. This meant that the residents of the area had to endure a five-hour power cut. It was hot, it was dark, and it was going to be for a while. What did we have to sacrifice for a wider common good? We sacrificed the things associated with electricity that our ancestors did not have in the first place, and found life meaningful all the same. They were happy with so much less. Can we do the same?

For us, no electricity may mean no air conditioning or fans, no television, DVD, computer or cordless telephones, no fridge, no washer, no dryer, no stove for some, no water supply for others, and no electric light. What does one do in order to survive such a drastic change in lifestyle?

Open windows and pray that it does not rain and that some breeze will blow. What about our brothers and sisters in the community who have to pull in shutters every night with little ventilation? We may use cell phones or phones that work even without electricity. What percentage of our people has no phone at home? Do you know? Many go to the laundromat to wash, while others wash on their hands and hang the clothes inside or outside to dry. Without a microwave or stove, we may have to cook outside. We call it barbecuing. Perhaps we will look into boiling contraptions for outdoors and smokers to cure our meat. For light, we use lanterns, lamps, candles and flash lights if we have enough kerosene or lamp oil, matches and batteries. When all is calculated and compared, we too can survive. The question is: will we be able to be happy and satisfied?

That evening of the power cut, we spent much of the time driving around, visiting a few friends, and talking together in the car, in the kitchen when we returned and in the bedrooms. Sharing limited light sources encouraged us to gather in one room. Talking together strengthened family ties, and going to bed earlier than usual rested the body. There are blessings to be found in any situation if we can focus on the bare essentials, and be creative and resourceful. In the end, we accepted what we could not change and tried to stay calm and even-tempered.

God wants us to be more grateful for each blessing that we do have, even as we may pray for improved circumstances. The bare essentials of your spiritual life (prayer, scripture, worship, service, fellowship) are intended to be in place all the time, so that no matter what else is added, or subtracted, you will not only survive but thrive. The danger comes when we allow the non-essential, transitory, temporary things of life to take the place of the essentials that are really indispensable. How well can you tell the difference?

YOUR REFLECTIONS

Chapter Nine
IGNITING THE PASSION FOR LIFELONG LEARNING

To Ignite

Several years ago the national theme for the school year was "Igniting the Passion for Life-long Learning". It still is an energy-filled and forward thinking approach to education.

To ignite something is to set it on fire. If you are burning a pile of bush, you have to start in a small section and let it spread slowly. If you put it in a container then you sprinkle the whole thing with a little kerosene and then light it after it has soaked. There are at least these two possibilities as an educational approach. Some hope that interest will develop as the child progresses through the school system without too much effort. Others want to "soak" the children with prayer, lectures, parental supervision, and intense teacher instruction on the value of striving for excellence, and the cultivation of self-motivated study habits. A combination of the two probably works the best, but some children do not respond well to pressure at an early age.

To ignite something requires the presence of fire in the first place. This means that someone has to already be on fire to produce such an effect. The many teacher-oriented seminars which are planned at the beginning of the school year are intended to inspire the administration, teaching, and support staff to become aglow with hopeful expectations for the year, and shine with the brightness of love and devotion.

What a wonderful thing it would be for our schools to so be aflame each year with discipline and dedication that all students had no choice but to respond. Can you imagine what it would be like to teach in a school where every child was truly interested in every subject, and discussed the lessons with a burning zeal to grasp every concept? How exciting to come home to a house where homework is done upon arrival from school because the student is impatient to complete the assignment in good time.

How nationally beneficial it would be if every child were to be in school every day of the school year, remaining in high school until graduation day, and gaining a four point average whenever possible. What would it mean to the work force, to have people who are on fire with the desire to make every business prosper if they are on staff, to make their chosen profession or vocation a source of personal gain and communal prosperity?

The Holy Spirit has been sent to ignite us every day with the will to love and serve God. When we are ignited with a strong faith, everything we do will radiate the heat of conviction, and we will automatically set our world on fire for change.

*Igniting The **Passion** for Life-long Learning*

How do we ignite passion in someone else? How do we stimulate an intense attachment to the good, the right, the desirable, and the worthwhile? According to St. Paul it is a matter of the mind, to begin to think in a particular fashion. In order to fight apathy, we have to train our minds to fight lethargic attitudes based on spirit-wearying thoughts. We have to oppose the pull to be lazy or satisfied with mediocrity. We have to decide that a particular standard needs to be maintained by us and apply ourselves to achieve this goal.

If we want children who are passionate about life, then we are called to model the same. They are more likely to reflect such energy and enthusiasm if they hear and see us focused on pursuing worthwhile dreams, discussing self-developing alternatives, and applying ourselves to wisdom consistently.

If we wake up in the morning and talk about our plans for the day with excitement, if we speak positively about the people with whom we work, or at best, with prayerful speculation about the work we hope that God is doing to bring out the best in them, they will be more inclined to follow suit.

Can you ignite anyone with your passion for the profitable? Is your passion consuming you because it is misdirected or out of control? The word passion can mean suffering as in the Holy Week accounts or it can also have sexual overtones when used in the context of romance. What we are referring to here is a strong love that is willing to suffer if need be but is deriving great benefit and pleasure from the activity pursued. This is passion at its best. It is a Spirit-led approach to life that perseveres in adversity, and is contagious in its effect. Our passion to please God with gratitude for blessings received prevents us from being selfish while our compassion for others keeps us from thinking too highly of ourselves.

Look around you and if you see someone who seems discouraged, or someone falling by the wayside, ignite the passion for living by introducing them to Jesus Christ. If they are disillusioned by their suffering, re-introduce them to the passages which speak of hope for the future, support in the present, God's faithfulness in the past. Ignite someone's passion for God today.

Igniting the Passion for What? If a love is so passionate for another that it becomes obsessive, that is a dangerous thing. If we are not able to release someone who wants to be free from us, we may be overly consumed by a human relationship that is standing in the way of our need for God. If a love for a cause is so passionate that we are prepared to utilize any means to justify the end, then we are in trouble if it leads us to contravene divine law. We cannot compromise our moral and ethical standards to beat an opponent, make a point, or obtain elusive goals. Our dreams have to be realized by methods that keep our integrity intact.

The love of freedom so fills the human spirit that people brave the desert, the sea, the snow and other treacherous conditions to find a better life. It has to be a strong pull to survive that makes refugees brave the unknown. It is a bright hope that lures many to leave home to seek to make their fortune in the world.

Several years ago, we in the Bahamas met face to face the force of the passion for religious ideals and political pronouncements. September 11th is a date that will remain with all of us who live in close proximity to the USA and are old enough to remember the terrorist attacks on the World Trade Centre and the Pentagon. When passion has a purpose it possesses a driving force that can change the world forever. This is why it is so important to know whether the object of our passion is worth the power to be expended.

We have to be very careful that when we ignite passion, we direct it toward the purpose for which we have been created, which is to live in harmony with one another as a result of our peace with God. Since God's goal is for us to be saved, then the passion or suffering of our Lord was the price God was willing to pay.

What are you passionate about and who benefits from the power you display? Are we blessed by your passion or is society disadvantaged by the object of your animated interests? A passion for pornography, a propensity for violence, an addiction to the destructive, these are like sticks of dynamite in the passenger section of a plane. We have no way of escape from being human, as we are all in flight toward a heavenly goal. Let your passion drive us to draw nearer to God.

Igniting The Passion For ***Life-Long*** *Learning*

If we look at the word "life-long" this means that time will not decrease its importance or reduce our passion. What do you intend to spend your life doing? How have you spent your years so far? How far are you along in gaining some of your goals and obtaining your objectives?

The image of climbing the ladder of success, rung by rung, presupposes that you are fully convinced that the effort expended is worth it, and the top of the ladder is desirable. The thought that it may be leaning against the wrong wall when we finally get to the top, challenges us to examine each step along the way to see if we are sure that this is how we want to invest our time and energy.

Those who drop out of school have decided that the educational ladder is not going to produce the results that they want in the time-frame it takes to achieve them. They may see themselves slipping backwards and switch to the ladder of early employment, or illegal acquisition of gain.

Those who devote themselves to a life of crime have decided that the status quo does not offer desired rewards to everyone equally, or that it operates its own form of organized crime. Perhaps, it is just a great game to get off with something for nothing. What a waste of wonderful human resources that could go into building up others rather than tearing down. How much further we could be if we all pulled together looking out for each other's good.

Choosing a career is quite a challenge if one expects to spend a life-time pursuing it. Choosing a life partner requires much prayer and dialogue if one plans to remain married to the same person until "death us do part."

We do not know how long we have to live, we are well aware of that. We presume we will grow old but there is no guarantee for that, or we may already be living so dangerously that we do not expect a long life span.

Since each day is "the present", each life is precious, and each path is undetermined, let us spend time alone in the quiet to decide how we will spend this day, in what we will invest our precious time, and in what direction we are moving as the days go by.

A lifetime may be a long time or a short time. It all boils down to a succession of "now times". Use your "now time" to help you to come into your prime, in each season of your life-time.

Igniting the Passion for Life-long ***Learning***

To learn is to acquire a new skill, realize a new truth, to be empowered to do more than we could before, or to do less to reduce our stress. I am thinking that perhaps I need to add Spanish to my language learning even though I completed Advanced Level French. I am told that it is the language of the region along with English. Those of you who are not at the stage of memory lapse need to avail yourselves of every opportunity that presents itself to be multi-lingual to cope with the coming decades.

I started to begin my piano lessons again after a lapse of thirty-something years. I say "started to begin" because I have since slowed the pace to less than a trickle. One day, I will play the hymns and spiritual songs close to my heart. Some time ago, my vegetable garden became a newly acquired possession after hurricane Floyd prepared the spot for me by physically removing the Poor Man's Orchard tree. Years later, my amateur efforts actually "bear fruit".

What have you been discovering this past week? Do you read in order to learn or do you listen to tapes? Are you enrolled in a course or have you just completed one? Do you talk to engaging people and listen to what their passion is, and how they seek to direct it? Do you travel when you can to places near and far, or watch a travel channel to travel without a passport?

Are you adding new recipes, experimenting with new hairstyles, making new friends, developing hidden talents, thinking new thoughts?

Let us avail ourselves of the many institutions of higher learning. Let us follow a dream, sharpen a skill, broaden our minds as best we can while we are still of sound mind. Our teachers can't do it alone. For our children to be excited about learning, ignite them in our homes, in the church, everywhere, by modelling an example of life-long learning that God has designed to last until the Lord comes again.

Again, I say, if we want our children to be ignited passionately to learn all of their lives, then we have to model the joy of learning at whatever stage we are. You can 'teach an old dog new tricks' if the Holy Spirit is the trainer-- so what are we waiting for?

YOUR REFLECTIONS

Chapter Ten
BECOMING MORE

Becoming More Prepared

There are definite advantages to listening attentively to others. One such advantage is that a listening attitude enables us to have an attitude of preparedness. It is as if you are preparing for something to come that is not yet known to you, but you want to be able to move into action at a moment's notice.

How can you become more prepared for the brighter future that God wants to give us even if it includes obstacles or outright suffering? The brightness of your "star shine" may need the backdrop of nighttime to reveal your true radiance. The way you carry your cross may be the witness of hope for thousands who are faltering in their faith.

What can you do to prepare for a future that you cannot see? Well, what about looking at your defenses? How do you handle change now? How eagerly do you welcome God doing a new thing in your life? What if you begin to prepare for interruptions in your schedule? As Bob Harrison says, he leaves spaces in his day schedule for interruptions so that something may be given more time, or for something totally unplanned to be introduced.

Prepare yourself to be enlightened by God. Read a book or the Bible with the expectation of a fresh revelation that could radically change your life or at least open your eyes to new methods or perspectives. Listening is using your ears to discern. Reading involves your eyes in the search for hidden truths. Read widely so that you will be able to discuss a wide variety of subjects. Your business or ministry, your counselling and teaching, your essays and papers, your class contributions and romantic relationships can all be enhanced by the wealth of knowledge you possess as a result of your taking advanced initiative to be prepared.

Prepare yourself for future employment by learning several skills that interest you if the opportunities present themselves. Learn how to do basic mechanic work to fix simple things in your car. Learn how to do simple carpentry, and other relatively easy repair jobs so that you can save money in the future. Learn how to budget your money from a computer program, friends who have the skill, or by an introductory course in accounting.

If you are still in school take different subjects that you can do well in and not take the easy way out. It is easier to learn new things while you are quite young. Practice your typing, become comfortable with computers, look at the jobs advertised in the newspapers and consider being re-trained before you become redundant if your current job is not secure.

Most of all, sit and quietly reflect on your strengths, list them, and pursue interests to develop them. Be prepared for God to reveal to you the work that you have been born to do, bearing in mind that it may change over the years. Be prepared by overcoming complacency and inviting God's creativity to control your life.

Becoming More Alert

To be alert to opportunity requires you to listen for the whisper of God in the words of others, and to be prepared for interruptions. The battle has been won if you are already prepared in your mind to be used, or to be transferred, or to be chosen by God to do a particular thing.

Your alertness is your way of keeping your preparations current. It is not that you are restless but that you complete your present assignments with the exactness that accompanies a possibly imminent departure. If you leave your home every day prepared for the possibility of guests accompanying you home in the evening, then you will be alert to hospitality opportunities because you are not hesitant to extend an unplanned invitation.

Of course your family needs to be in agreement with interruption as a blessing rather than a curse, or the ensuing tension will charge the atmosphere and make sensitive guests very uncomfortable. Taking the family and guests out to eat may be a better solution if all are not prepared, or if the home is likely to be in a state of disarray upon your return.

Your alertness is reflected in having several books in your locker at school so that home work may be done while you wait for your transportation after school, even if the class was not the same day. Alertness is keeping an umbrella handy that is light weight or a plastic poncho or rain coat that folds down to a very small size, so that you are able to prepare for bad weather as soon as it threatens, particularly if you walk, take the bus, or park some distance from your destination.

Alertness is how a dog looks when its ears are both straight up even if it is lying down. The faintest sound is to be decoded in case action is necessary. Listen and prepare for life, listening for God-sent signals, even as we wait for hurricane alerts when a storm has been sighted.

Alertness is recognizing the moods of parents, teachers, supervisors or bosses, and treading more carefully so that care will be taken to prevent conflict. There is no need to endure a war that could easily have been avoided. Do not aggravate the powerful unless God sends you on a specific mission like David to Goliath. Similarly, parents, 'do not provoke your children' is in the Bible, and it may be expanded to teachers and students, employers and employees as well. Provocation is the making of excessive demands, conflict initiation through persecution, or some other unreasonable attitude that pushes a less powerful person to rebel.

Be alert to the first signs of the winds of change, and see if you are being called by God to participate. "Here am I, send me" is the alert response to an unexpected request by one who is both listening and prepared. How alert are you?

Becoming More Responsive

Those who are alert are in a position to respond as soon as the alarm is sounded, a suggestion made, a request uttered, or a command is given. The one who listens will hear, the one who is prepared and alert can act without hesitation.

If you received a sudden invitation to an event that would put you in contact with people who may advance your cause, expand your ministry or business, put you in line for a college scholarship or bless you in some way, would you be able to accept on the spur of the moment? Do you have at least one outfit in your wardrobe so that you would not decline because you do not have the time to go shopping?

Do you have a few dollars saved somewhere safe (preferably the bank) so that you may take advantage of a window of opportunity that is opening, but needs a little seed money to get things started? Can you say no to non-essentials so that you may respond to an excellent offer?

Is your resume or curriculum vitae updated sufficiently that you would be able to go for a job interview tomorrow, respond to a college opportunity with current transcripts or letters of recommendation? Are your passport and driver's license renewed so that you can travel abroad in an emergency or to accept a trip as a gift with short notice? How much notice do you need to respond to one of God's great deals? Could you relocate by having your essential papers and items handy as Mary and Joseph had to do if your house should catch on fire?

Are your nets mended so that Jesus can tell you where to fish? Is your boat in good shape so that Jesus could choose to teach from your vessel? Would you lend your donkey and colt without having to delay Jesus' entry into Jerusalem by having to take time to make up your mind? Are you fit enough to run to the tomb if Mary told you about the resurrection of Jesus from the dead? Are you ready to yell out to Jesus to heal your blindness as you sit begging beside the road? Is your gratitude such that you would remember to come back to Jesus to say thank you for healing your leprosy? Would you be willing to stop as the Samaritan did and help someone without dragging your feet, or regretting your decision to "not get involved", after you gave it some thought miles down the road?

Stay alert so that you can respond. Scripture is full of people who seized the moment. Even though Jesus may be on his way to raise a dead girl, reach out and touch the hem of his garment and be healed. If you see his feet need washing, get out your perfume and use your hair to dry them or whatever you have that is your pride and joy. Roll out your Persian carpet for his donkey to ride on, give him your loaves and fish, your Johnny cake and boiled fish to feed some hungry people. Respond today to some need God will bring your way.

Becoming More Disciplined

To hold on to your promising present, you need to exercise self-discipline over the long haul. The brighter future will one day present itself to you as the realized present, because you listened, prepared, were alert and responsive.

In order to keep it from being your dazzling past, you want to maintain your hold on the treasure in your hand, and keep God's blessings current.

Do not become lazy or complacent, do not cease to listen or keep preparing, do not become indifferent and no longer alert so that you are not able to respond as new opportunities present themselves. God is always creating something new, always looking for a fresh canvas on which to paint a new vision, always reaching out in love to unrepentant sinners.

If you do not remain vigilant with your healthy eating habits, you will put weight on, and lose your muscle tone if you neglect your exercise routine. Spiritually, you will retreat rather than advance, if you are not spending time in daily prayer, study of God's word, worship, connection to a christian community and serving the Lord somehow. Short periods of interruption may occur, but that is to be a noticeable exception that reinforces your need to re-establish the pattern of spiritual discipline as soon as possible.

Discipline, young people, is the training of yourself to keep doing what is right, what you need to do rather than what you want to do. Your approach to your room now, whether you keep it tidy or at least are able to find your things when you need them right away may be an indication as to how you will keep your office later, how you will handle your finances and even your spiritual and moral life. Your attitude to homework may make the difference between getting a college degree or failing because you could not meet the deadlines for your assignments, if there were parties to attend. Learning to keep curfew now helps you to come home after work later on when you have a family that needs your time and attention.

Discipline for all adults is the attention to details in relationships so that they please God, and in finances so that we avoid bankruptcy or unnecessary hand-to-mouth living. It is focusing on priorities and keeping them present in each day's schedule. It is allowing the Holy Spirit to remain in control. It is on-going training for fuller Christ-likeness.

Discipline is celebrating life that is free from uninvited wicked witches, as in the fairy tales, who try to put us to sleep for a hundred years, so as to freeze our productivity, cramp our creativity, hinder our prosperity, and decrease our spirituality. Let the Holy Spirit keep you on the cutting edge of cultural change and tribal transformation. No more narrow-minded self-centeredness, it is time for a Christ-centered miracle mind-set. Listen, prepare, stay alert and respond. Be disciplined and before long your bright future will be shining right here in the palm of your hand.

YOUR REFLECTIONS

Chapter Eleven
GETTING DOWN TO BUSINESS

The Business Plan

I consulted a bright young businessman to get his views on how to make a new business develop into a great business. Over the next few days, I hope that we will also apply some of the principles to the business of serving the Lord, by building up God's kingdom at the same time.

I was told that "prior to starting any business, it is essential to create a road map or a business plan." It is a way of measuring the proposed growth and the desired means of achieving it. The documentation of abstract thoughts allows the team to understand the dream or vision and to make suggestions for refining the methodology.

In the scripture, we find God's business plan with its outline of the plan of salvation and obedient service. The more familiar we are with the details, the better able we are to appreciate the plan and absorb ourselves in executing it with precision.

Do you have a plan for your business that is clear and identifiable by all involved? Do you have a plan for your family, with recognizable goals and obvious guidelines? Do you have a plan for your life? Is it one which you have allowed to shape and mould you with divine wisdom, or did you trust your own judgment to work it all out, in spite of your limited perception of future developments?

It is like having a study plan in order to complete the preparation in time to sit the examinations. It is like a pilot's flight plan that determines direction and destination and permits the necessary contacts to be made with the respective airport towers.

I hope that your plans will be in the best interest of both your business and your family. Time needs to be effectively allocated to achieve several desirable goals at the same time. God's plan has blessings in it for everyone. There is room for every person on this planet to find a place in this plan. It involves obedience so that nothing will distract us from the highest calling of our lives. If you are drifting aimlessly, or your boat is rocking violently, give your rudder and your wheel to the Lord and it will never again be business as usual.

Management

A talented management team has the responsibility of developing and executing strategies and decisions to promote the success of a business. Every organization needs to have a group of people with skills for leadership to remain alert to all that the plan requires.

Once the plan is in place the management team must track actual performance against the plan. Whenever the expected results are not achieved, it then permits speedy detection and rectification of the situation. The trend has to be revised quickly in order to keep the plan on track.

The same is true for our personal lives. The more we examine our actual performance against the Lord's example of a holy and God-pleasing lifestyle, the more quickly we detect sin and redirect our course.

It requires much honesty and some time expended to access the spiritual damage that different decisions make. How well are you measuring up to your plans for a mature, well rounded and exemplary lifestyle?

More than this daily determination of success and fortune, the committed christian needs to follow the example of those in business who actively engage in forecasting to discover whether the cumulative effect of a sequence of actions is likely to fall below, meet or exceed expectations. In other words, are you going to really "miss the mark" this year (which is one of the definitions of sin), or are you actually getting closer to becoming the person that you think that God would have you become?

If sin is interpreted as a moral or spiritual deficit, then it is sound business practice and wise spiritual practice to use cash management strategies that match output with income. Debt is giving out what you do not have in your account, using an overdraft facility to try and remain afloat which, with high interest rates, may erode all profits. Similarly, we need to be putting into our lives the spiritual reserves that we have to draw on, on a daily basis.

Wisdom, patience, joy, love, hope and faith are just some of the withdrawals that need to be made from your inner resources: putting in time to pray, worship, study, minister to others, to be counselled and given spiritual direction, are the deposits that will keep your spiritual bank account "in the black" instead of "in the red".

What do you need to put in place today to help you get back on track with the plan that you know will bring you maximum benefits? Make the adjustments as needed and then expect to see the character of Christ emerge in yourself gradually, as you get back on the "good foot".

Paying Attention

More wise words came in the form of an emphasis on paying attention to the needs and issues of your staff and customers. Follow the temperature in the room, in the meeting, in the corridors, to give you an indication of how "hot under the collar" people are getting. Some disastrous situations may be circumvented if you give others an opportunity to express what the experience is doing to them.

In the same way, every family has a thermometer or barometer, and even the youngest child has a contribution to make to the harmony or discord in a home. Each church has its own issues, and we all do well to keep our finger on the pulse of any organization or establishment to see what signs of built up pressure are becoming evident.

God has given us several indicators to reveal to us that we are deviating from a wholesome design for christian living. Psychosomatic illness indicates that feelings remain unaddressed. Headaches and indigestion may point to mounting pressure in the mind. Waking several times through the night, or insomnia, may reveal that the time has come to make some definite decisions that have spiritual and moral implications.

Just as a good business team monitors trends in industry and products consumed, so the christian must look for changes in the needs of those around, and share the gospel in an appropriate manner to attract attention to God's plan as the best one possible. A close assessment of inventory turnover exposes the flaws in marketing if an item is not being promoted well, or the decrease in demand and the need to shift stock intake.

If we want to build up God's kingdom we have to look at what we are teaching, how we are preaching and how accessible is our location. Our comfort is not the key. We are not in it for us. We are here to do God's will and what we seek to measure is not as easy as performing inventory counts and comparing them to perpetual records, but God will reveal to us where changes need to be made, if we are humble enough to ask and to listen to the response.

Each of us has certain strengths and weaknesses, and we have particular gifts for ministry. Perhaps we need to spend more time matching our gifts to particular needs so that we narrow our product base, as it were, before engaging in the expansion of our personal product lines. When we pool all of our resources, using all of our God-given gifts, each of God's customers will be well served.

Capital and Markets

If money is needed to undergird a business so that it will not fail because it is inadequately capitalized, then the power of the Holy Spirit is the capital that every christian needs to succeed in the business of witnessing for the Lord. Once the capital is well managed it is important to look at the primary target market.

Just as the advertiser uses techniques that will attract a particular clientele, so too there is an approach to evangelism that is like the right key in the correct door. Demographics such as age, gender and class distinctions have long shaped how a product is marketed. Advertising cigarettes while in the fresh mountain air, or while on horseback, gives the feeling that it is not really an act of pollution. The smoke is hardly noticeable in that setting. Isn't it interesting that such commercials are seldom in smoky joints with cigarette butts and dark circles under card-playing people's eyes? No "lady of the night" promotes their product on the screen. They look for young professionals to suggest prosperity and sophistication. With all of the Surgeon General's warnings it seems that overt advertisement has been severely curtailed or eliminated altogether.

What about the ads for alcoholic beverages? Seldom would they warn that the over use of the product leads to accidents and show a drunk-driver in a traffic mishap. No obvious alcoholic is contracted to welcome the next generation to join the many persons who are in a living death because of addiction. Instead, the association is with the lithe and lovely, or the erotic and extravagant, the partying crowd or "jet set," as we used to call them. The call is to relax, unwind and have a good time using this beverage as a means of being socially accepted and even sexually attractive.

We want to help our people to beware of the pitfalls of addiction to a substance that can wreak havoc on this nation. Some may use moderation well, but others find it beyond their strength. Too many drink too much.

We have to promote drinking from the fountain of life, and relaxing in the peace of prayer. We want to target the market of our children, youth and young adults to consider a drug-free and sexually inactive lifestyle. We need to talk more about how God provides for our needs, how God helps us to exercise self-restraints in any area of challenge. If we know the plan, and we are on the team to go out and make disciples, then how well do we package our product to attract the attention of our primary target market – our nation's youth?

YOUR REFLECTIONS

THE VINE AND THE BRANCHES

[1]"I am the true vine, and my Father is the gardener.

[2]He cuts off every branch in me that bears no fruit, while every branch that does bear fruit he prunes so that it will be even more fruitful.

[3]You are already clean because of the word I have spoken to you.

[4]Remain in me, and I will remain in you. No branch can bear fruit by itself; it must remain in the vine. Neither can you bear fruit unless you remain in me.

(John 15:1-4 NIV)